ANIMALS
That Make a Difference!

Beavers

Ashley Lee

Explore other books at:
WWW.ENGAGEBOOKS.COM

VANCOUVER, B.C.

e➚ WWW.ENGAGEBOOKS.COM

Beavers: Level 2
Animals That Make a Difference!
Lee, Ashley 1995 –
Text © 2020 Engage Books
Design © 2020 Engage Books

Edited by: A.R. Roumanis,
Jared Siemens, and Lauren Dick
Design by: A.R. Roumanis

Text set in Arial Regular.
Chapter headings set in Arial Black.

FIRST EDITION / FIRST PRINTING

LIBRARY AND ARCHIVES CANADA CATALOGUING IN PUBLICATION

Title: Beavers: Animals That Make a Difference Level 2 reader / Ashley Lee
Names: Lee, Ashley, 1995- author

Identifiers: Canadiana (print) 20200308920 | Canadiana (ebook) 20200308939
ISBN 978-1-77437-636-2 (hardcover)
ISBN 978-1-77437-637-9 (softcover)
ISBN 978-1-77437-638-6 (pdf)
ISBN 978-1-77437-639-3 (epub)
ISBN 978-1-77437-640-9 (kindle)

Subjects:
LCSH: Beavers—Juvenile literature
LCSH: Human-animal relationships—Juvenile literature

Classification: LCC QL737.R632 L44 2020 | DDC J599.37—DC23

Contents

4 What Are Beavers?

6 A Closer Look

8 Where Do Beavers Live?

10 What Do Beavers Eat?

12 How Do Beavers Talk to Each Other?

14 Beaver Life Cycle

16 Curious Facts About Beavers

18 Kinds of Beavers

20 How Beavers Help
    Other Animals

22 How Beavers
    Help Earth

24 How Beavers
    Help Humans

26 Beavers in Danger

28 How To Help Beavers

30 Quiz

What Are Beavers?

Beavers are the second largest **rodents** on Earth. They are related to rats and squirrels.

KEY WORD

Rodents: warm-blooded animals with bones in their backs. They have long, sharp front teeth.

Beavers are known for their building skills. They are one of the only animals that can change their **environment**. This is very helpful to people, other animals, and Earth.

KEY WORD

Environment: the physical surroundings of a person, plant, or animal.

5

A Closer Look

A beaver can be up to 4 feet (1.3 meters) long with its tail stretched out.

Beavers have long, flat tails that are covered in scales. This tail helps beavers swim and keep their balance.

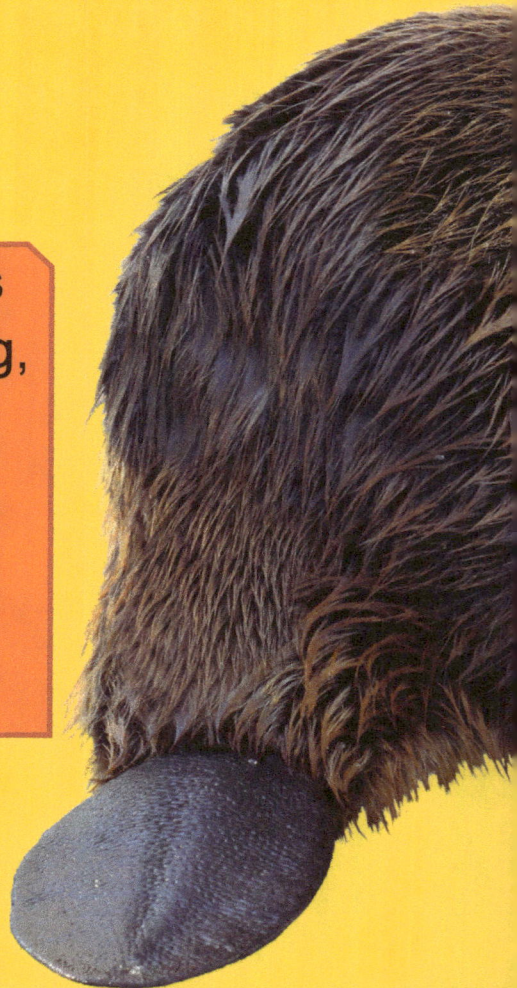

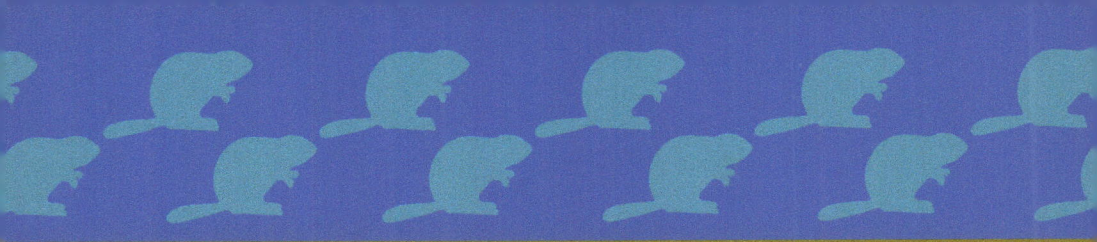

Beavers have long front teeth that never stop growing. Chewing wood stops them from getting too big.

Beavers have back feet that are webbed. This makes them excellent swimmers.

Where Do Beavers Live?

Beavers create dams from mud and branches to stop flowing water. This creates a pond. Beavers build houses called lodges on the ponds they create.

KEY WORD

Habitats: the places a plant or animal lives. Different animals need different habitats.

Beavers live in Northern parts of the world. The North American beaver lives in North America. The European beaver lives in Europe and northern Asia. They live in forest habitats near water.

Europe

Arctic Ocean

Europe

Asia

Atlantic Ocean

North America

North America

Africa

Northern Asia

South America

Pacific Ocean

Southern Ocean

Antarctica

0   2,000 miles

0   4,000 kilometers

N

Legend
- Land
- Ocean

What Do Beavers Eat?

Beavers are **herbivores**. They eat plants, twigs, and tree bark.

KEY WORD

Herbivores: animals that only eat plants. They do not eat meat.

Lodges give beavers access to water plants. This is helpful in winter when food is hard to find on land.

How Do Beavers Talk to Each Other?

Beavers make many different noises to talk to their family members. They rarely make noise outside of their lodges.

Beavers make a smelly liquid called castor. This tells other animals to stay away. They build piles of dirt and leaves around their home and cover them in castor.

Beavers will sometimes slap their tails on the water to warn others of danger.

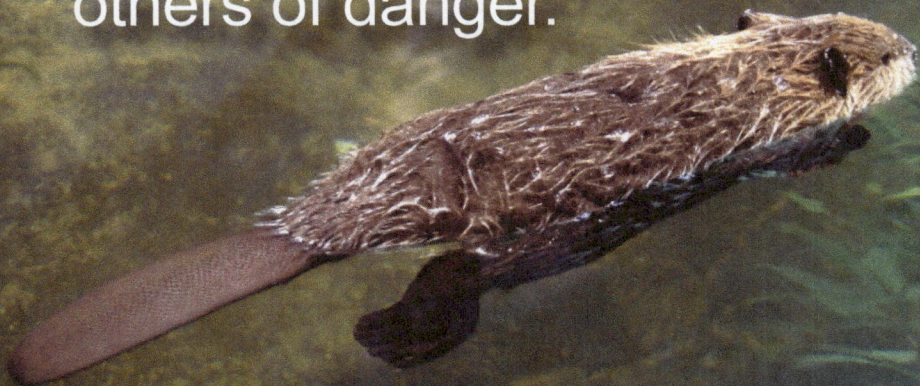

Beaver Life Cycle

Beavers are social animals. They live together in groups called colonies. These groups are usually made up of two adults and their babies.

Baby beavers are called kits. They learn to swim when they are only one month old.

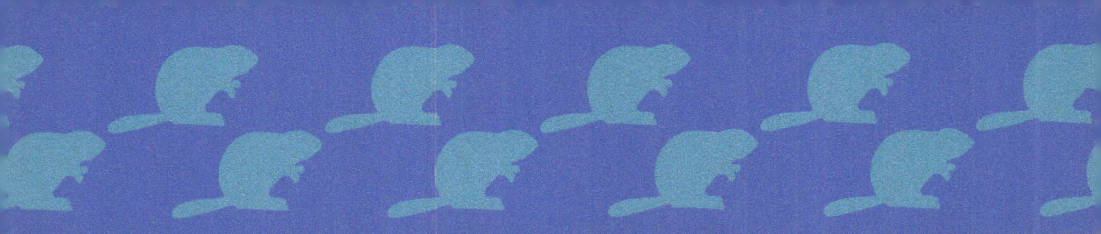

Young beavers leave home when they are around two years old.

Beavers live to be about 12 years old. They spend their lives working together to create big, strong lodges.

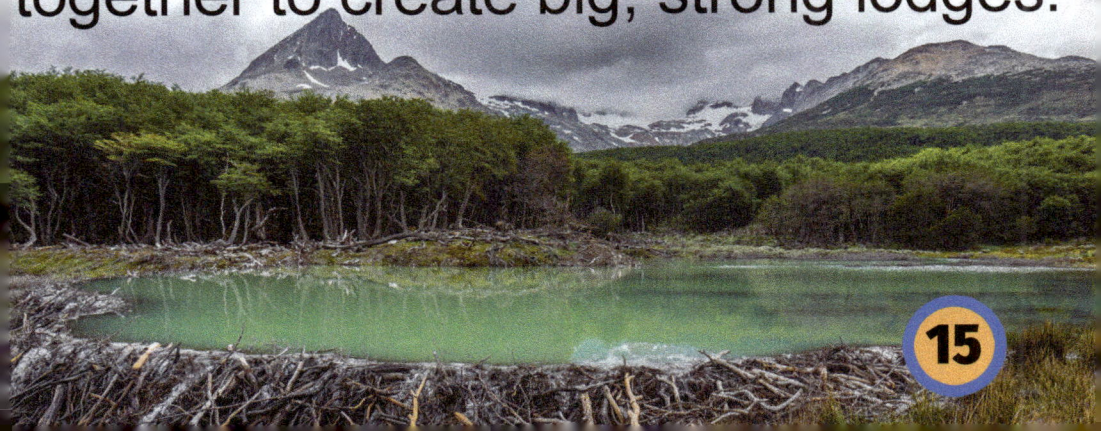

Curious Facts About Beavers

Beavers have a chemical in their teeth that makes them orange.

Beavers have a set of clear eyelids. This helps them see underwater without hurting their eyes.

Beavers can stay underwater for up to 15 minutes.

16

Beavers sometimes share their lodges with other animals like muskrats, otters, and turtles.

Many beavers are nocturnal. This means they sleep during the day and work at night.

The world's largest beaver dam is in Alberta, Canada. It is almost 2,800 feet (850 m) long!

Kinds of Beavers

There are only two kinds of beavers. The North American beaver and the European beaver look very similar. There are ways to tell them apart.

North American beavers have wide tails. Their heads are large and square.

European beaver tails are not as wide as those of North American beavers. These beavers have smaller heads that are triangle shaped.

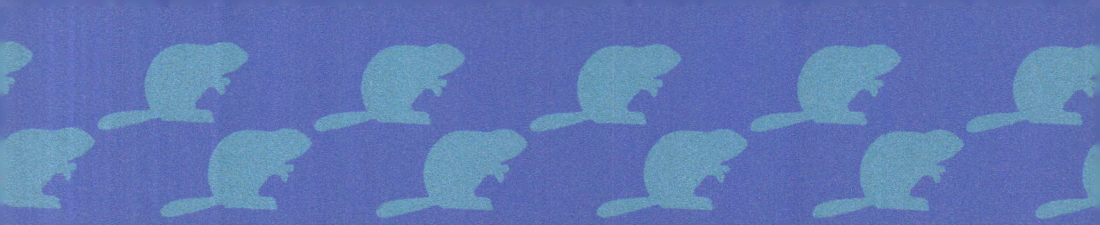

How Beavers Help Other Animals

Beavers make habitats better for other animals. Their ponds provide drinking water. They cut down trees that then grow new leaves. These leaves are food for moose and elk.

Scientists have found that there are more animals in areas with beavers. Beavers have helped bring back animals to areas they had disappeared from.

How Beavers Help Earth

Wildfires often happen in dry areas. Beaver dams keep the area around them wet. This can help prevent wildfires from spreading.

Beaver dams help keep water clean. They slow the flow of water and act like a filter. The dams catch dirt and **pollution** and stop it from reaching other places.

KEY WORD

Pollution: harmful waste that enters an environment. Garbage and chemicals can both cause pollution.

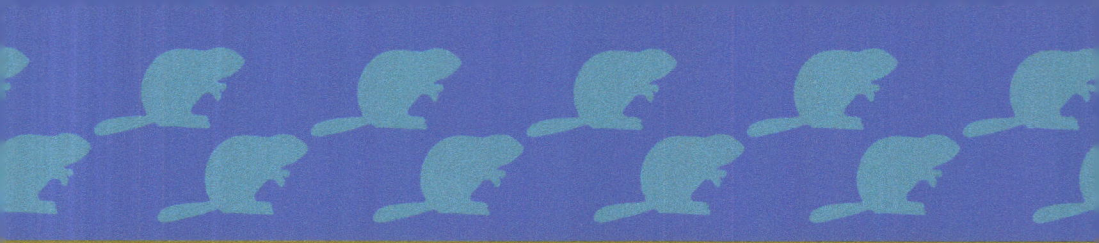

How Beavers Help Humans

Beaver dams can help stop flooding in towns and farms. Their dams slow the flow of water. This stops large amounts of water from coming in at once.

Beavers help keep water clean. This includes water that humans use every day for drinking, bathing, and watering crops.

Beavers in Danger

Beavers were hunted for their fur for almost 250 years. They became endangered. This means there were very few of them left.

Beavers are not endangered anymore. Many beavers lose their homes as people build bigger cities. They can easily become endangered again if they continue to lose their homes.

How To Help Beavers

The best way to help beavers is to keep rivers, streams, and lakes clean. This will keep beaver dams and lodges clean.

Many people plan river clean-ups with their friends and family. Clean habitats can encourage young beavers to make homes in new places.

Quiz

Test your knowledge of beavers by answering the following questions. The questions are based on what you have read in this book. The answers are listed on the bottom of the next page.

1 What are baby beavers called?

2 How long do beavers live?

3 How long can beavers stay underwater?

4 What other animals do beavers share their lodges with?

5 How many types of beavers are there?

6 What can help stop flooding in towns and farms?

Explore other books in the Animals That Make a Difference series.

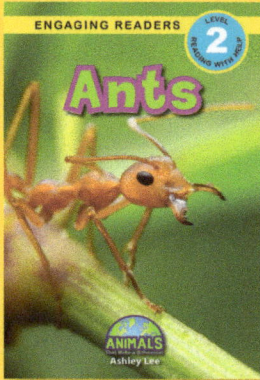

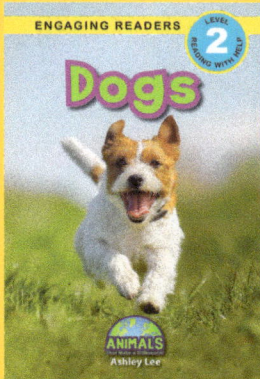

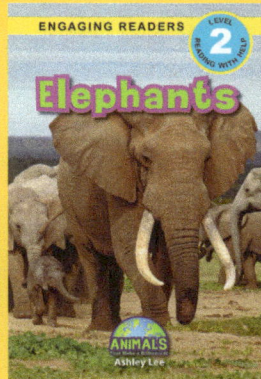

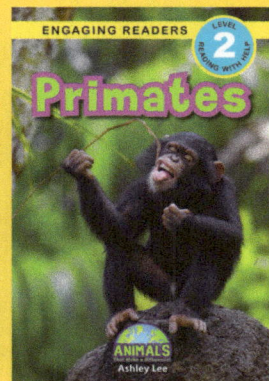

Visit www.engagebooks.com to explore more Engaging Readers.

Answers: 1. Kits 2. About 12 years 3. Up to 15 minutes 4. Muskrats, otters, and turtles 5. Two 6. Beaver dams

www.ingramcontent.com/pod-product-compliance
Lightning Source LLC
Chambersburg PA
CBHW051234020426
42331CB00016B/3376